THE ART OF VIRTUE

THE ART OF VIRTUE

Ben Franklin's Formula for
Successful Living

BENJAMIN FRANKLIN

Skyhorse Publishing

Skyhorse Publishing books may be purchased in bulk at special discounts for sales promotion, corporate gifts, fund-raising, or educational purposes. Special editions can also be created to specifications. For details, contact the Special Sales Department, Skyhorse Publishing, 307 West 36th Street, 11th Floor, New York, NY 10018 or info@skyhorsepublishing.com.

Skyhorse® and Skyhorse Publishing® are registered trademarks of Skyhorse Publishing, Inc.®, a Delaware corporation.

Visit our website at www.skyhorsepublishing.com

10 9 8 7 6 5 4 3 2 1

Library of Congress Cataloging-in-Publication Data is available on file.

ISBN: 978-1-61608-331-1

Printed in China

CONTENTS

THE ART OF VIRTUE

At the time I established myself in Pennsylvania, there was not a good bookseller's shop in any of the colonies to the southward of Boston. In New York and Philadelphia, the printers were indeed stationers; but they sold only paper, almanacs, ballads, and a few common school-books. Those who loved reading were obliged to send for their books from England; the members of the Junto had each a few. We had left the ale-house, where we first met, and hired a room to hold our club in. I proposed that we should all of us bring our books to that room, where they would not only be ready to consult in our conferences, but become a common benefit, each of us being at liberty to borrow such as he wished to read at home. This was accordingly done, and for some time contented us.

Finding the advantage of this little collection, I proposed to render the benefit from the books more common, by commencing a public subscription library. I drew a sketch of the plan and rules that would be necessary, and got a skilful conveyancer, Mr. Charles Brockden, to put the whole in form of articles of agreement to be subscribed; by which each subscriber engaged to pay a certain sum down for the first purchase of the books, and an annual contribution for increasing them. So few were the readers at that time in Philadelphia, and the majority of us so poor, that I was not able with great industry to find more than fifty persons, mostly young tradesmen, willing to pay down for this purpose forty shillings each, and ten shillings per annum. With this little fund we began. The books were imported. The library was opened one day in the week for lending them to subscribers, on their promissory notes to pay double the value if not duly returned. The institution soon manifested its utility, was imitated by other towns, and in other provinces. The libraries were augmented by donations, reading became fashionable; and our people having no public amusements to divert their attention from study, became better acquainted with books, and in a few years were observed by strangers to be better instructed and more intelligent than people of the same rank generally are in other countries.

When we were about to sign the above-mentioned articles, which were to be binding on us, our heirs, &c., for fifty years, Mr. Brockden, the scrivener, said to us, "You are young men, but it is scarcely probable that any of you will live to see the expiration of the term fixed in the instrument." A number of us, however, are yet living; but the instrument was after a few years rendered null, by a charter that incorporated and gave perpetuity to the company.

The objections and reluctances I met with in soliciting the subscriptions made me soon feel the impropriety of presenting one's self as the proposer of any useful project that might be supposed to raise one's reputation in the smallest degree above that of one's neighbors, when one has need of their assistance to accomplish that project. I therefore put myself as much as I could out of sight, and stated it as a scheme of a *number of friends*, who had requested me to go about and propose it to such as they thought lovers of reading. In this way my affair went on more smoothly, and I ever afterwards practiced it on such occasions; and, from my frequent successes, can heartily recommend it. The present little sacrifice of your vanity will afterwards be amply repaid. If it remains a while uncertain to whom the merit belongs, some one more vain than yourself may be encouraged to claim it, and then even envy will be disposed to do you justice, by plucking those assumed feathers, and restoring them to their right owner.

This library afforded me the means of improvement by constant study, for which I set apart an hour or two each day, and thus repaired in some degree the loss of the learned education my father once intended for me. Reading was the only amusement I allowed myself. I spent no time in taverns, games, or frolics of any kind; and my industry in my business continued as indefatigable as it was necessary. I was indebted for my printing-house; I had a young family coming on to be educated, and I had two competitors to contend with for business who were established in the place before me. My circumstances, however, grew daily easier. My original habits of frugality continuing, and my father having, among his instructions to me when a boy, frequently repeated a proverb of Solomon, "*Seest thou a man diligent in his calling, he shall stand before kings, he shall not stand before mean men*," I thence considered industry as a means of obtaining wealth and distinction, which encouraged me, though I did not think that I should ever literally *stand before kings*, which however has since happened; for I have stood before *five*, and even had the honor of sitting down with one, the King of Denmark, to dinner.

We have an English proverb that says, "*He that would thrive must ask his wife.*" It was lucky for me that I had one as much disposed to industry and frugality as myself. She assisted me cheerfully in my business, folding and stitching pamphlets, tending shop, purchasing old linen rags for the paper-makers, &c. We kept no idle servants, our table was plain and simple, our furniture of the cheapest. For instance, my breakfast was for a long time bread and milk (no tea), and I ate it out of a two-penny earthen porringer, with a pewter spoon. But mark how luxury will enter families, and make a progress, in spite of principle; being called one morning to breakfast, I found it in a china bowl, with a spoon of silver! They had been bought for me without my knowledge by my wife, and had cost her the enormous sum of three-and-twenty shillings; for which she had no other excuse or apology to make, but that she thought *her* husband deserved a silver spoon and china bowl as well as any of his neighbors. This was the first appearance of plate and china in our house; which after-wards, in a course of years, as our wealth increased, augmented gradually to several hundred pounds in value.

I had been religiously educated as a Presbyterian; but, though some of the dogmas of that persuasion, such as the *eternal decrees of God, election, reprobation, &c.*, appeared to me unintelligible, others doubtful, and I early absented myself from the public assemblies of the sect, Sunday being my studying day, I never was without some religious principles. I never doubted, for instance, the existence of a Deity—that he made the world and governed it by his providence—that the most acceptable service of God was the doing good to man; that our souls are immortal; and that all crimes will be punished, and virtue rewarded, either here or hereafter. These I esteemed the essentials of every religion; and, being to be found in all the religions we had in our country, I respected them all, though with different degrees of respect, as I found them more or less mixed with other articles, which, without any tendency to inspire, promote, or confirm morality, served principally to divide us, and make us unfriendly to one another. This respect to all, with an opinion that the worst had some good effects, induced me to avoid all discourse that might tend to lessen the good opinion another might have of his own religion; and as our province increased in people, and new places of worship were continually wanted, and generally erected by voluntary contribution, my mite for such purpose, whatever might be the sect, was never refused.

Though I seldom attended any public worship, I had still an opinion of its propriety, and of its utility, when rightly conducted, and I regularly paid my annual subscription for the support of the only Presbyterian minister or meeting we had in Philadelphia. He used to visit me sometimes as a friend, and admonish me to attend his administrations; and I was now and then prevailed

on to do so; once for five Sundays successively. Had he been in my opinion a good
preacher, perhaps I might have continued,
notwithstanding the occasion I had for the
Sunday's leisure in my course of study; but
his discourses were chiefly either polemic
arguments or explications of the peculiar
doctrines of our sect, and were all to me very
dry, uninteresting, and unedifying; since not
a single moral principle was inculcated or
enforced, their aim seeming to be rather to
make us *Presbyterians* than *good citizens.*

At length he took for his text that verse
of the fourth chapter to the Philippians,
"*Finally, brethren, whatsoever things are
true, honest, just, pure, lovely, or of good
report, if there be any virtue, or any praise,
think on these things.*" And I imagined, in
a sermon on such a text, we could not miss
of having some morality. But he confined
himself to five points only, as meant by the
apostle:

1. Keeping holy the Sabbath day.

2. Being diligent in reading the Holy Scriptures.

3. Attending duly the public worship.

4. Partaking of the Sacrament.

5. Paying a due respect to God's ministers.

These might be all good things; but, as they were not the kind of good things that I expected from that text, I despaired of ever meeting with them from any other, was disgusted, and attended his preaching no more. I had some years before composed a little liturgy, or form of prayer, for my own private use (in 1728), entitled *Articles of Belief and Acts of Religion.* I returned to the use of this, and went no more to the public assemblies. My conduct might be blamable, but I leave it, without attempting further to excuse it; my present purpose being to relate facts, and not to make apologies for them.

It was about this time I conceived the bold and arduous project of arriving at *moral perfection*. I wished to live without committing any fault at any time, and to conquer all that either natural inclination, custom, or company might lead me into. As I knew, or thought I knew, what was right and wrong, I did not see why I might not *always* do the one and avoid the other. But I soon found I had undertaken a task of more difficulty than I had imagined. While my attention was taken up, and care employed, guarding against one fault, I was often surprised by another; habit took the advantage of inattention; inclination was sometimes too strong for reason. I concluded, at length, that the mere speculative conviction, that it was our interest to be completely virtuous was not sufficient to prevent our slipping; and that the contrary habits must be broken, and good ones acquired and established, before we can have any dependence on a steady, uniform rectitude of conduct. For this purpose I therefore tried the following method.

In the various enumerations of the *moral virtues* I had met with in my reading, I found the catalogue more or less numerous, as different writers included more or fewer ideas under the same name. *Temperance*, for example, was by some confined to eating and drinking; while by others it was extended to mean the moderating every other pleasure, appetite, inclination, or passion, bodily or mental, even to our avarice and ambition. I proposed to myself, for the sake of clearness, to use rather more names, with fewer ideas annexed to each, than a few names with more ideas; and I included under thirteen names of virtues all that at that time occurred to me as necessary or desirable; and annexed to each a short precept, which fully expressed the extent I gave to its meaning. These names of *virtues*, with their precepts, were:

1. Temperance
Eat not to dullness; drink not to elevation.

2. Silence
Speak not but what may benefit others or yourself; avoid trifling conversation.

3. Order
Let all your things have their places; let each part of your business have its time.

4. Resolution
Resolve to perform what you ought; perform without fail what you resolve.

5. Frugality
Make no expense but to do good to others or yourself; that is, waste nothing.

6. Industry
Lose no time; be always employed in something useful; cut off all unnecessary actions.

7. Sincerity
Use no hurtful deceit; think innocently and justly; and, if you speak, speak accordingly.

8. Justice
Wrong none by doing injuries, or omitting the benefits that are your duty.

9. Moderation
Avoid extremes; forbear resenting injuries so much as you think they deserve.

10. Cleanliness
Tolerate no uncleanliness in body, clothes, or habitation.

11. Tranquiility
Be not disturbed at trifles, or at accidents common or unavoidable.

12. Chastity
Rarely use venery but for health or offspring—never to dullness, weakness, or

the injury of your own or another's peace or reputation.

13. HUMILITY
Imitate Jesus and Socrates.

My intention being to acquire the *habitude* of all these virtues, I judged it would be well not to distract my attention by attempting the whole at once, but to fix it on *one* of them at a time; and, when I should be master of that, then to proceed to another; and so on, till I should have gone through the thirteen. And, as the previous acquisition of some might facilitate the acquisition of certain others, I arranged them with that view, as they stand above. *Temperance* first, as it tends to procure that coolness and clearness of head, which is so necessary where constant vigilance was to be kept up, and a guard maintained against the unremitting attraction of ancient habits, and the force of perpetual temptations. This being acquired and established, *Silence* would be more easy; and my desire being to gain knowledge, at the same time that I improved in virtue, and considering that in conversation it was obtained rather by the use of the ear than of the tongue, and therefore wishing to break a habit I was getting into of prattling, punning, and jesting, which only made me acceptable to trifling company, I gave *Silence* the second place. This and the next, *Order*, I expected, would allow me more time for attending to my project and my studies. *Resolution*, once become habitual, would keep me firm in my endeavors to obtain all the subsequent virtues; *Frugality* and *Industry* relieving me from my remaining debt, and producing affluence and independence, would make more easy the practice of *Sincerity* and *Justice*, &c., &c. Conceiving then, that, agreeably to the advice of Pythagoras in his *Golden Verses*, daily examination would be necessary, I contrived the following method for conducting that examination.

I made a little book, in which I allotted a page for each of the virtues. I ruled each page with red ink, so as to have seven columns, one for each day of the week, marking each column with a letter for the day. I crossed these columns with thirteen red lines, marking the beginning of each line with the first letter of one of the virtues; on which line, and in its proper column, I might mark, by a little black spot, every fault I found upon examination to have been committed respecting that virtue, upon that day.

I determined to give a week's strict attention to each of the virtues successively. Thus, in the first week, my great guard was to avoid every the least offence against *Temperance*, leaving the other virtues to their ordinary chance, only marking every evening the faults of the day. Thus, if in the first week I could keep my first line, marked T, clear of spots, I supposed the habit of that virtue so much strengthened, and its opposite weakened, that I might venture extending my attention to include the next, and for the following week keep both lines clear of spots. Proceeding thus to the last, I could get through a course complete in thirteen weeks, and four courses in a year. And like him, who, having a garden to weed, does not attempt to eradicate all the bad herbs at once, which would exceed his reach and his strength, but works on one of the beds at a time, and, having accomplished the first, proceeds to a second; so I should have, I hoped, the encouraging pleasure of seeing on my pages the progress made in virtue by clearing successively my lines of their spots, till in the end, by a number of courses, I should be happy in viewing a clean book after a thirteen weeks' daily examination.

This my little book had for its motto, these lines from Addison's *Cato*:

> "Here will I hold. If there's a power above us,

(And that there is all nature cries aloud
Through all her works). He must delight
in virtue;
And that which He delights in must be
happy."

Another from Cicero:

"O vitæ Philosophia dux! O virtutum
indagatrix expultrixque vitiorum!
Unus dies, bene et ex pracæptis tuis
actus, peccanti immortalitati est ante-
ponendus."

Another from the Proverbs of Solomon,
speaking of wisdom or virtue:

"Length of days is in her right hand, and
in her left hand riches and honour.
Her ways are ways of pleasantness.
and all her paths are peace."

And conceiving God to be the fountain of
wisdom, I thought it right and necessary

to solicit His assistance for obtaining it; to this end I formed the following little prayer, which was prefixed to my tables of examination, for daily use.

> "O powerful Goodness! bountiful Father! merciful Guide! Increase in me that wisdom which discovers my truest interest. Strengthen my resolution to perform what that wisdom dictates. Accept my kind offices to Thy other children, as the only return in my power for Thy continual favors to me."

I used also sometimes a little prayer which I took from Thomson's *Poems*, viz.:

> "Father of light and life, Thou Good Supreme!
> O teach me what is good; teach me Thyself!
> Save me from folly, vanity, and vice,
> From every low pursuit; and feed my soul

With knowledge, conscious peace, and
    virtue pure;
Sacred, substantial, never-fading bliss!"

I entered upon the execution of this plan
for self-examination, and continued it with
occasional intermissions for some time. I
was surprised to find myself so much fuller
of faults than I had imagined; but I had the
satisfaction of seeing them diminish. To
avoid the trouble of renewing now and then
my little book, which, by scraping out the
marks on the paper of old faults, to make
room for new ones in a new course, became
full of holes, I transferred my tables and
precepts to the ivory leaves of a memorandum
book, on which the lines were drawn with
red ink, that made a durable stain; and on
those lines I marked my faults with a black-
lead pencil, which marks I could easily wipe
out with a wet sponge. After a while I went
through one course only in a year, and after-

wards only one in several years, till at length I omitted them entirely, being employed in voyages and business abroad with a multiplicity of affairs, that interfered; but I always carried my little book with me.

My scheme of *Order* gave me the most trouble: and I found that, though it might be practicable where a man's business was such as to leave him the disposition of his time, that of a journeyman printer for instance, it was not possible to be exactly observed by a master, who must mix with the world, and often receive people of business at their own hours. Order, too with regard to places for things, papers, &c., I found extremely difficult to acquire. I had not been early accustomed to method, and, having an exceedingly good memory, I was not so sensible of the inconvenience attending want of method. This article, therefore, cost me much painful attention, and my faults in it vexed me so

much, and I made little progress in amend-
ment, and had such frequent relapses, that I
was almost ready to give up the attempt, and
content myself with a faulty character in that
respect. Like the man who, in buying an axe
of a smith, my neighbor, desired to have the
whole of its surface as bright as the edge. The
smith consented to grind it bright for him,
if he would turn the wheel; he turned, while
the smith pressed the broad face of the axe
hard and heavily on the stone, which made
the turning of it very fatiguing. The man
came every now and then from the wheel
to see how the work went on, and at length
would take his axe as it was, without further
grinding. "No," said the smith, "turn on,
turn on, we shall have it bright by and by; as
yet it is only speckled." "Yes," said the man,
"but *I think I like a speckled axe best.*" And
I believe this may have been the case with
many, who, having for want of some such
means as I employed, found the difficulty of

obtaining good and breaking bad habits in other points of vice and virtue, have given up the struggle, and concluded that "a *speckled axe is best*." For something, that pretended to be reason, was every now and then suggesting to me, that such extreme nicety as I exacted of myself might be a kind of foppery in morals, which, if it were known, would make me ridiculous; that a perfect character might be attended with the convenience of being envied and hated; and that a benevolent man should allow a few faults in himself, to keep his friends in countenance.

In truth, I found myself incorrigible with respect to *Order*; and now I am grown old, and my memory bad, I feel very sensibly the want of it. But on the whole, though I never arrived at the perfection I had been so ambitious of obtaining, but fell far short of it, yet I was, by the endeavor, a better and a happier man than I otherwise should have been, if

I had not attempted it; as those who aim at perfect writing by imitating the engraved copies, though they never reach the wished-for excellence of those copies, their hand is mended by the endeavor, and is tolerable while it continues fair and legible.

It may be well my posterity should be informed, that to this little artifice, with the blessing of God, their ancestor owed the constant felicity of his life, down to his seventy-ninth year, in which this is written. What reverses may attend the remainder is in the hand of Providence; but, if they arrive, the reflection on past happiness enjoyed ought to help his bearing them with more resignation. To *Temperance* he ascribes his long-continued health, and what is still left to him of a good constitution; to *Industry* and *Frugality*, the early easiness of his circumstances and acquisition of his fortune, with all the knowledge that enabled him to be a useful citizen, and obtained for him some degree of reputation among the learned; to *Sincerity* and *Justice*, the confidence of his country, and the honourable employs it conferred upon him; and to the joint influence of the whole mass of the virtues, even in the imperfect state he was able to acquire them, all that evenness of temper, and that cheerfulness in conversation, which makes his company still sought for, and agreeable even to his young acquaintance. I hope, therefore, that some of my descendants may follow the example and reap the benefit.

It will be remarked that, though my scheme was not wholly without religion, there was in it no mark of any of the distinguishing tenets of any particular sect. I had purposely avoided them; for, being fully persuaded of the utility and excellency of my method, and that it might be serviceable to people in all religions, and intending some time or other to publish it, I would not have anything in it that should prejudice any one, of any sect, against it. I proposed writing a little comment on each virtue, in which I would have shown the advantages of possessing it, and the mischiefs attending its opposite vice; I should have called my book THE ART OF VIRTUE, because it would have shown the means and manner of obtaining virtue, which would have distinguished it from the mere exhortation to be good, that does not instruct and indicate the means; but is like the Apostle's man of verbal charity, who, without showing to the naked and hungry, how or where they might get clothes or victuals, only exhorted them to be fed and clothed. *James* ii. 15, 16.

But it so happened, that my intention of writing and publishing this comment was never fulfilled. I had, indeed, from time to time, put down short hints of the sentiments and reasonings to be made use of in it; some of which I have still by me; but the necessary close attention to private business in the earlier part of life, and public business since, have occasioned my postponing it. For, it being connected in my mind with *a great and extensive project*, that required the whole man to execute, and which an unforeseen succession of employs prevented my attending to, it has hitherto remained unfinished. In this piece it was my design to explain and enforce this doctrine, *that vicious actions are not hurtful because they are forbidden, but forbidden because they are hurtful*, the nature of man alone considered; that it was, therefore, every one's interest to be virtuous, who wished to be happy even in this world; and I should from this circumstance (there being always in the world a number of rich merchants, nobility, states, and princes, who have need of honest instruments for the management of their affairs, and such being so rare) have endeavoured to convince young persons, that no qualities are so likely to make a poor man's fortune, as those of *probity* and *integrity*.

My list of virtues contained at first but twelve; but a Quaker friend having kindly informed me, that I was generally thought proud; that my pride showed itself frequently in conversation; that I was not content with being in the right when discussing any point, but was overbearing, and rather insolent, of which he convinced me by mentioning several instances; I determined to endeavour to cure myself, if I could, of this vice or folly among the rest; and I added *Humility* to my list, giving an extensive meaning to the word.

I cannot boast of much success in acquiring the *reality* of this virtue, but I had a good deal with regard to the appearance of it. I made it a rule to forbear all direct contradiction to the sentiments of others, and all positive assertion of my own. I even forbid myself, agreeably to the old laws of our Junto, the use of every word or expression in the language that imported a fixed opinion; such as *certainly, undoubtedly,* &c., and I adopted instead of them, I *conceive,* I *apprehend,* or I *imagine,* a thing to be so or so; or it so *appears to me at present.* When another asserted something that I thought an error, I denied myself the pleasure of contradicting him abruptly, and of showing immediately some absurdity in his proposition; and in answering I began by observing, that, in certain cases or circumstances, his opinion would be right, but in the present case there *appeared* or seemed to me some difference, &c. I soon found the advantage of this change in my manners; the conversations I engaged in went on more pleasantly. The modest way in which I proposed my opinions procured them a readier reception and less contradiction; I had less mortification when I was found to be in the wrong; and I more easily prevailed with others to give up their mistakes and join with me, when I happened to be in the right.

And this mode, which I at first put on with some violence to natural inclination, became at length easy, and so habitual to me, that perhaps for the last fifty years no one has ever heard a dogmatical expression escape me. And to this habit (after my character of integrity) I think it principally owing, that I had early so much weight with my fellow-citizens, when I proposed new institutions or alterations in the old; and so much influence in public councils, when I became a member; for I was but a bad speaker, never eloquent, subject to much hesitation in my choice of words, hardly correct in language, and yet I generally carried my point.

In reality there is, perhaps, no one of our natural passions so hard to subdue as *pride*. Disguise it, struggle with it, stifle it, mortify it as much as one pleases, it is still alive, and will every now and then peep out and show itself; you will see it, perhaps, often in this history. For, even if I could conceive that I had completely overcome it, I should probably be *proud* of my *humility*.

———

Let no pleasure tempt thee, no profit allure thee, no ambition corrupt thee, no example sway thee, no persuasion move thee, to do any thing which thou knowest to be evil; so shalt thou always live jollily; for a good conscience is a continual Christmas.

On Beginning of Public Employment

Having mentioned a great and *extensive project*, which I had conceived, it seems proper that some account should be here given of that project and its object. Its first rise in my mind appears in the following little paper, accidentally preserved, viz.

"*Observations on my reading history in the Library, May 9th, 1731.*

"That the great affairs of the world, the wars and revolutions, are carried on and effected by parties.

"That the view of these parties is their present general interest, or what they take to be such.

"That the different views of these different parties occasion all confusion.

"That while a party is carrying on a general design, each man has his particular private interest in view.

"That as soon as a party has gained its general point, each member becomes intent upon his particular interest; which, thwarting others, breaks that party into divisions and occasions more confusion.

"That few in public affairs act from a mere view of the good of their country, whatever they may pretend; and, though their actings bring real good to their country, yet men primarily considered that their own and their country's interest were united, and so did not act from a principle of benevolence.

"That fewer still in public affairs act with a view to the good of mankind.

"There seems to me at present to be great occasion for raising a *United Party for*

Virtue, by forming the virtuous and good men of all nations into a regular body, to be governed by suitable good and wise rules, which good and wise men may probably be more unanimous in their obedience to than common people are to common laws.

"I at present think that whoever attempts this aright, and is well qualified, cannot fail of pleasing God and of meeting with success."

Revolving this project in my mind, as to be undertaken hereafter, when my circumstances should afford me the necessary leisure, I put down from time to time on pieces of paper such thoughts as occurred to me respecting it. Most of these are lost; but I find one purporting to be the substance of an intended creed, containing, as I thought, the essentials of every known religion, and being free of everything that might shock the professors of any religion. It is expressed in these words, viz.

"That there is one God, who made all things.

"That he governs the world by his providence.

"That he ought to be worshipped by adoration, prayer, and thanksgiving.

"But that the most acceptable service to God is doing good to man.

"That the soul is immortal.

"And that God will certainly reward virtue and punish vice, either here or hereafter."

My ideas at that time were, that the sect should be begun and spread at first among young and single men only; that each person to be initiated should not only declare his assent to such creed, but should have exercised himself with the thirteen weeks' examination and practice of the virtues, as in the before-mentioned model; that the existence of such a society should be kept a secret, till it was become considerable, to prevent solicitations for the admission of improper persons; but that the members should, each of them, search among his acquaintance for ingenious, well-disposed youths, to whom, with prudent caution, the scheme should be gradually communicated. That the members should engage to afford their advice, assistance, and support to each other in promoting one another's interest, business, and advancement in life. That for distinction, we should be called THE SOCIETY OF THE FREE AND EASY. Free, as being, by the general practice and habits of the virtues, free from the dominion of vice; and particularly, by the practice of industry and frugality, free from debt, which exposes a man to constraint, and a species of slavery to his creditors.

This is as much as I can now recollect of the project, except that I communicated it in part to two young men, who adopted it with some enthusiasm; but my then narrow circumstances, and the necessity I was under of sticking close to my business, occasioned my postponing the further prosecution of it at that time; and my multifarious occupations, public and private, induced me to continue postponing, so that it has been omitted, till I have no longer strength or activity left sufficient for such an enterprise. Though I am still of opinion it was a practicable scheme, and might have been very useful, by forming a great number of good citziens; and I was not discouraged by the seeming magnitude of the undertaking, as I have always thought, that one man of tolerable abilities may work great changes, and accomplish great affairs among mankind, if he first forms a good plan; and, cutting off all amusements or other employments, that would divert his attention, makes the execution of that same plan his sole study and business.

In 1732, I first published my Almanac, under the name of *Richard Saunders*; it was continued by me about twenty-five years, and commonly called *Poor Richard's Almanac*. I endeavoured to make it both entertaining and useful, and it accordingly came to be in such demand, that I reaped considerable profit from it; vending annually near ten thousand. And observing that it was generally read, scarce any neighborhood in the province being without it, I considered it as a proper vehicle for conveying instruction among the common people, who bought scarcely any other books. I therefore filled all the little spaces, that occurred between the remarkable days in the Calendar, with proverbial sentences, chiefly such as incul-cated industry and frugality, as the means of procuring wealth, and thereby securing virtue; it being more difficult for a man in want to act always honestly, as, to use here one of those proverbs, *it is hard for an empty sack to stand upright.*

These proverbs, which contained the wisdom of many ages and nations, I assembled and formed into a connected discourse prefixed to the Almanac of 1757, as the harangue of a wise old man to the people attending an auction. The bringing all these scattered counsels thus into a focus enabled them to make greater impression. The piece, being universally approved, was copied in all the newspapers of the American continent, reprinted in Britain on a large sheet of paper, to be stuck up in houses; two translations were made of it in France, and great numbers bought by the clergy and gentry, to distribute gratis among their poor parishioners and tenants. In Pennsylvania, as it discouraged useless expense in foreign superfluities, some thought it had its share of influence in producing that growing plenty of money, which was observable for several years after its publication.

I considered my newspaper, also, as another means of communicating instruction, and in that view frequently reprinted in it extracts from the *Spectator*, and other moral writers; and sometimes published little pieces of my own, which had been first composed for reading in our Junto. Of these are a Socratic dialogue, tending to prove that, whatever might be his parts and abilities, a vicious man could not properly be called a man of sense; and a discourse on self-denial, showing that virtue was not secure, till its practice became a *habitude*, and was free from the opposition of contrary inclinations. These may be found in the papers about the beginning of 1735.

In the conduct of my newspaper, I carefully excluded all libelling and personal abuse, which is of late years become so disgraceful to our country. Whenever I was solicited to insert anything of that kind, and the writers pleaded, as they generally did, the liberty of the press; and that a newspaper was like a stagecoach, in which any one who would pay had a right to a place; my answer was, that I would print the piece separately if desired, and the author might have as many copies as he pleased to distribute himself; but that I would not take upon me to spread his detraction; and that, having contracted with my subscribers to furnish them with what might be either useful or entertaining, I could not fill their papers with private altercation, in which they had no concern, without doing them manifest injustice. Now, many of our printers make no scruple of gratifying the malice of individuals, by false accusations of the fairest characters among ourselves, augmenting animosity even to the producing of duels; and are, moreover, so indiscreet as to print scurrilous reflections on the government of neighboring states, and even on the conduct of our best national allies, which may be attended with the most pernicious consequences. These things I mention as a caution to young printers, and that they may be encouraged not to pollute their presses, and disgrace their profession by such infamous practices, but refuse steadily; as they may see by my example, that such a course of conduct will not on the whole be injurious to their interests.

In 1733, I sent one of my journeymen to Charleston, South Carolina, where a printer was wanting. I furnished him with a press and letters, on an agreement of partnership, by which I was to receive one-third of the profits of the business, paying one-third of the expense. He was a man of learning, but ignorant on matters of account; and, though he sometimes made me remittances, I could get no account from him, nor any satisfactory state of our partnership while he lived. On his decease, the business was continued by his widow, who, being born and bred in Holland, where, as I have been informed, the knowledge of accounts makes a part of female education, she not only sent me as clear a statement as she could find of the transactions past, but continued to account with the greatest regularity and exactness every quarter afterwards; and managed the business, with such success, that she not only reputably brought up a family of children, but, at the expiration of the term, was able to purchase of me the printing-house, and establish her son in it.

I mention this affair chiefly for the sake of recommending that branch of education for our young women, as likely to be of more use to them and their children, in case of widowhood, than either music or dancing; by preserving them from losses by imposition of crafty men, and enabling them to continue, perhaps, a profitable mercantile house, with established correspondence, till a son is grown up fit to undertake and go on with it; to the lasting advantage and enriching of the family.

About the year 1734, there arrived among us a young Presbyterian preacher, named Hemphill, who delivered with a good voice, and apparently extempore, most excellent discourses; which drew together consider-able numbers of different persuasions, who joined in admiring them. Among the rest, I became one of his constant hearers, his sermons pleasing me, as they had little of the dogmatical kind, but inculcated strongly the practice of virtue, or what in the religious style are called *good works*. Those, however, of our congregation, who considered them-selves as orthodox Presbyterians, disap-proved his doctrine, and were joined by most of the old ministers, who arraigned him of heterodoxy before the synod, in order to have him silenced. I became his zealous partisan, and contributed all I could to raise a party in his favour, and combated for him awhile with some hopes of success. There was much scribbling *pro* and *con* upon the occasion; and finding that, though an elegant preacher, he was but a poor writer, I wrote for him two or three pamphlets, and a piece in the *Gazette* of April, 1735. Those pamphlets, as is generally the case with controversial writings, though eagerly read at the time, were soon out of vogue, and I question whether a single copy of them now exists.

During the contest an unlucky occurrence hurt his cause exceedingly. One of our adversaries having heard him preach a sermon, that was much admired, thought he had somewhere read the sermon before, or at least a part of it. On searching, he found that part quoted at length, in one of the British *Reviews* from discourse of Dr. Foster's. This detection gave many of our party disgust, who accordingly abandoned his cause and occasioned our more speedy discomfiture in the synod. I stuck by him, however; I rather approved his giving us good sermons composed by others, than bad ones of his own manufacture; though the latter was the practice of our common teachers. He afterwards acknowledged to me, that none of those he preached were his own; adding, that his memory was such as enabled him to retain and repeat any sermon after once reading only.

On our defeat, he left us in search elsewhere of better fortune, and I quitted the congregation, never attending it after; though I continued many years my subscription for the support of its ministers.

After ten years' absence from Boston, and having become easy in my circumstances, I made a journey thither to visit my relations; which I could not sooner afford. In returning I called at Newport to see my brother James, then settled there with his printing-house.

Our former differences were forgotten, and our meeting was very cordial and affectionate. He was fast declining in health, and requested me that, in case of his death, which he apprehended was not far distant, I would take home his son, then but ten years of age, and bring him up to the printing business. This I accordingly performed; sending him a few years to school before I took him into the office. His mother carried on the business till he was grown up, when I assisted him with an assortment of new types, those of his father being in a manner worn out. Thus it was that I made my brother ample amends for the service I had deprived him of by leaving him so early.

In 1736 I lost one of my sons, a fine boy of four years old, by the smallpox, taken in the common way. I long regretted him bitterly, and still regret that I had not given it to him by inoculation. This I mention for the sake of parents who omit that operation on the supposition that they should never forgive themselves if a child died under it; my example showing that the regret may be the same either way, and therefore that the safer should be chosen.

Our club, the Junto, was found so useful, and afforded such satisfaction to the members, that some were desirous of introducing their friends, which could not well be done without exceeding what we had settled as a convenient number, viz., twelve. We had from the beginning made it a rule to keep our institution a secret, which was pretty well observed; the intention was to avoid applications of improper persons for admittance, some of whom, perhaps, we might find it difficult to refuse. I was one of those who were against any addition to our number, but instead of it made in writing a proposal that every member separately should endeavour to form a subordinate club, with the same rules respecting queries, etc., and without informing them of the connection with the Junto. The advantages proposed were the improvement of so many more young citizens by the use of our institutions; our better acquaintance with the general sentiments of the inhabitants on any occasion, as the Junto member might propose what queries we should desire, and was to report to the Junto what passed at his separate club; the promotion of our particular interests in business by more extensive recommendation, and the increase of our influence in public affairs, and our power of doing good by spreading through the several clubs the sentiments of the Junto.

The project was approved, and every member undertook to form his club; but they did not all succeed. Five or six only were completed, which were called by different names, as the *Vine*, the *Union*, the *Band*. They were useful to themselves, and afforded us a good deal of amusement, information, and instruction; besides answering, in some considerable degree, our views of influencing the public on particular occasions; of which I shall give some instances in course of time as they happened.

My first promotion was my being chosen, in 1736, clerk of the General Assembly. The choice was made that year without opposition; but the year following, when I was again proposed, the choice like that of the members being annual, a new member made a long speech against me, in order to favour some other candidate. I was however chosen, which was the more agreeable to me, as besides the pay for the immediate service of clerk, the place gave me a better opportunity of keeping up an interest among the members which secured to me the business of printing the votes, laws, paper-money, and other occasional jobs for the public, that on the whole were very profitable.

I therefore did not like the opposition of this new member, who was a gentleman of fortune and education, with talents that were likely to give him in time great influence in the House, which indeed afterwards happened. I did not, however, aim at gaining his favour by paying any servile respect to him, but, after some time, took this other method. Having heard that he had in his library a certain very scarce and curious book, I wrote a note to him, expressing my desire of perusing that book, and requesting that he would do me the favour of lending it to me for a few days. He sent it immediately; and I returned it in about a week with another note, expressing strongly the sense of the favour. When we next met in the House he spoke to me, which he had never done before, and with great civility; and he ever after manifested a readiness to serve me on all occasions, so that we became great friends, and our friendship continued to his death. This is another instance of the truth of an old maxim I had learned, which says: *"He that has once done you a kindness will be more ready to do you another, than he whom you yourself have obliged."* And it shows how much more profitable it is prudently to remove, than to resent, return, and continue, inimical proceedings.

In 1737, Colonel Spotswood, late governor of Virginia, and then postmaster-general, being dissatisfied with the conduct of his deputy at Philadelphia, respecting some negligence in rendering, and want of exactness in framing, his accounts, took from him the commission and offered it to me. I accepted it readily, and found it of great advantage; for, though the salary was small, it facilitated the correspondence that improved my newspaper, increased the number demanded, as well as the advertisements to be inserted, so that it came to afford me a considerable income. My old competitor's newspaper declined proportionably, and I was satisfied without retaliating his refusal, while postmaster, to permit my papers being carried by the riders. Thus he suffered greatly from his neglect in due accounting: and I mention it as a lesson to those young men, who may be employed in managing affairs for others, that, they should always render accounts, and make remittances, with great clearness and punctuality. The character of observing such a conduct is the most powerful of all recommendations to new employments and increase of business.

I began now to turn my thoughts to public affairs, beginning, however, with small matters. The city watch was one of the first things that I conceived to want regulation. It was managed by the constables of the respective wards in turn; the constable summoned a number of housekeepers to attend him for the night. Those who chose never to attend paid him six shillings a year to be excused, which was supposed to go to hiring substitutes, but was in reality much more than was necessary for that purpose, and made the constableship a place of profit; and the constable, for a little drink, often got such ragamuffins about him as a watch, that respectable housekeepers did not choose to mix with. Walking the rounds, too, was often neglected, and most of the nights spent in tippling. I thereupon wrote a paper to be read in the Junto, representing these irregularities, but insisting more particularly on the inequality of the six shilling tax of the constable, respecting the circumstances of those who paid it; since a poor widow housekeeper, all whose property to be guarded by the watch did not perhaps exceed the value of fifty pounds, paid as much as the wealthiest merchant, who had thousands of pounds' worth of goods in his stores.

On the whole I proposed as a more effectual watch, the hiring of proper men to serve constantly in the business; and as a more equitable way of supporting the charge, the levying a tax that should be proportioned to the property. This idea, being approved by the Junto, was communicated to the other clubs, but as originating in each of them; and though the plan was not immediately carried into execution, yet, by preparing the minds of the people for the change, it paved the way for the law obtained a few years after, when the members of our clubs were grown into more influence.

About this time I wrote a paper (first to be read in the Junto, but it was afterwards published) on the different accidents and carelessnesses by which houses were set on fire, with cautions against them, and means proposed of avoiding them. This was spoken of as a useful piece, and gave rise to a project, which soon followed it, of forming a company for the more ready extinguishing of fires, and mutual assistance in removing and securing of goods when in danger. Associates in this scheme were presently found amounting to thirty. Our articles of agreement obliged every member to keep always in good order, and fit for use, a certain number of leathern buckets, with strong bags and baskets (for packing and transporting of goods), which were to be brought to every fire; and we agreed about once a month to spend a social evening together, in discoursing and communicating such ideas as occurred to us upon the subject of fires as might be useful in our conduct on such occasions.

The utility of this institution soon appeared, and many more desiring to be admitted than we thought convenient for one company, they were advised to form another, which was accordingly done; and thus went on one new company after another, till they became so numerous as to include most of the inhabitants who were men of property; and now, at the time of my writing this, though upwards of fifty years since its establishment, that which I first formed, called the *Union Fire Company*, still subsists; though the first members are all deceased but one, who is older by a year than I am. The fines that have been paid by members for absence at the monthly meetings have been applied to the purchase of fire-engines, ladders, fire-hooks, and other useful implements for each company; so that I question whether there is a city in the world better provided with the means of putting a stop to beginning conflagrations; and, in fact, since these institutions, the city has never lost by fire more than one or two houses at a time, and the flames have often been extinguished before the house in which they began has been half consumed.

———

He that can compose himself, is wiser than he that composes books.

Learning, whether speculative or practical, is, in popular or mixt governments, the natural source of wealth and honour.

On Temperance

From his autobiography, pages 146–151

At my first admission into this printing-house I took to working at press, imagining I felt a want of the bodily exercise I had been us'd to in America, where presswork is mix'd with composing. I drank only water; the other workmen, near fifty in number, were great guzzlers of beer. On occasion, I carried up and down stairs a large form of types in each hand, when others carried but one in both hands. They wondered to see, from this and several instances, that the *Water-American*, as they called me, was *stronger* than themselves, who drank *strong* beer! We had an alehouse boy who attended always in the house to supply the workmen. My companion at the press drank every day a pint before breakfast, a pint at breakfast with his bread and cheese, a pint between breakfast and dinner, a pint at dinner, a pint in the afternoon about six o'clock, and another when he had done his day's work. I thought it a detestable custom; but it was necessary, he suppos'd, to drink *strong* beer, that he might be *strong* to labor. I endeavored to convince him that the bodily strength afforded by beer could only be in proportion to the grain or flour of the barley dissolved in the water of which it was made; that there was more flour in a pennyworth of bread; and therefore, if he would eat that with a pint of water, it would give him more strength than a quart of beer. He drank on, however, and had four or five shillings to pay out of his wages every Saturday night for that muddling liquor; an expense I was free from. And thus these poor devils keep themselves always under.

Watts, after some weeks, desiring to have me in the composing-room, I left the pressmen; a new bien venu or sum for drink, being five shillings, was demanded of me by the compositors. I thought it an imposition, as I had paid below; the master thought so too, and forbad my paying it. I stood out two or three weeks, was accordingly considered as an excommunicate, and had so many little pieces of private mischief done me, by mixing my sorts, transposing my pages, breaking my matter, etc., etc., if I were ever so little out of the room, and all ascribed to the chappel ghost, which they said ever haunted those not regularly admitted, that, notwithstanding the master's protection, I found myself oblig'd to comply and pay the money, convinc'd of the folly of being on ill terms with those one is to live with continually.

I was now on a fair footing with them, and soon acquir'd considerable influence. I propos'd some reasonable alterations in their chappel laws, and carried them against all opposition. From my example, a great part of them left their muddling breakfast of beer, and bread, and cheese, finding they could with me be suppyl'd from a neighboring house with a large porringer of hot water-gruel, sprinkled with pepper, crumb'd with bread, and a bit of butter in it, for the price of a pint of beer, viz., three half-pence. This was a more comfortable as well as cheaper breakfast, and kept their heads clearer. Those who continued sotting with beer all day, were often, by not paying, out of credit at the alehouse, and us'd to make interest with me to get beer; their *light,* as they phrased it, *being out.* I watch'd the pay-table on Saturday night, and collected what I stood engag'd for them, having to pay sometimes near thirty shillings a week on their accounts. This, and my being esteem'd a pretty good *riggite,* that is, a jocular verbal satirist, supported my consequence in the society. My constant attendance (I never making a St. Monday) recommended me to the master; and my uncommon quickness at composing occasioned my being put upon all work of dispatch, which was generally better paid. So I went on now very agreeably.

My lodging in Little Britain being too remote, I found another in Duke-street, opposite to the Romish Chapel. It was two pair of stairs backwards, at an Italian warehouse. A widow lady kept the house; she had a daughter, and a maid servant, and a journeyman who attended the warehouse, but lodg'd abroad. After sending to inquire my character at the house where I last lodg'd, she agreed to take me in at the same rate, 3s. 6d. per week; cheaper, as she said, from the protection she expected in having a man lodge in the house. She was a widow, an elderly woman; had been bred a Protestant, being a clergyman's daughter, but was converted to the Catholic religion by her husband, whose memory she much revered; had lived much among people of distinction, and knew a thousand anecdotes of them as far back as the times of Charles the Second.

She was lame in her knees with the gout, and, therefore, seldom stirred out of her room, so sometimes wanted company; and hers was so highly amusing to me, that I was sure to spend an evening with her whenever she desired it. Our supper was only half an anchovy each, on a very little strip of bread and butter, and half a pint of ale between us; but the entertainment was in her conversation. My always keeping good hours, and giving little trouble in the family, made her unwilling to part with me; so that, when I talk'd of a lodging I had heard of, nearer my business, for two shillings a week, which, intent as I now was on saving money, made some difference, she bid me not think of it, for she would abate me two shillings a week for the future; so I remained with her at one shilling and sixpence as long as I staid in London.

In a garret of her house there lived a maiden lady of seventy, in the most retired manner, of whom my landlady gave me this account: that she was a Roman Catholic, had been sent abroad when young, and lodg'd in a nunnery with an intent of becoming a nun; but, the country not agreeing with her, she returned to England, where, there being no nunnery, she had vow'd to lead the life of a nun, as near as might be done in those circumstances. Accordingly, she had given all her estate to charitable uses, reserving only twelve pounds a year to live on, and out of this sum she still gave a great deal in charity, living herself on water-gruel only, and using no fire but to boil it. She had lived many years in that garret, being permitted to remain there gratis by successive Catholic tenants of the house below, as they deemed it a blessing to have her there. A priest visited her to confess her every day. "I have ask'd her," says my landlady, "how she, as she liv'd, could possibly find so much employment for a confessor?" "Oh," said she, "it is impossible to avoid *vain thoughts.*" I was permitted once to visit her. She was chearful and polite, and convers'd pleasantly. The room was clean, but had no other furniture than a matras, a table with a crucifix and book, a stool which she gave me to sit on, and a picture over the chimney of Saint Veronica displaying her handkerchief, with the miraculous figure of Christ's bleeding face on it, which she explained to me with great seriousness. She look'd pale, but was never sick; and I give it as another instance on how small an income, life and health may be supported.

———

Drunkenness, that worst of Evils, makes some men Fools, some Beasts, some Devils.

When Wine enters, out goes the Truth.

On Silence and Moderation

From his autobiography, pages 419–426

To Arthur Lee, dated Passy, 4 April, 1778

Mr. Deane communicated to me his intentions of setting out for America immediately, as a secret, which he desired I would mention to nobody. I complied with his request. If he did not think fit to communicate it to you also, it is from him you should demand his reasons.

This court has an undoubted right to send as ministers whom it pleases, and where it pleases, without advising with us, or desiring our approbation. The measure of sending M. Gérard as a minister to Congress was resolved on without consulting me; but I think it a wise one, and, if I did not, I do not conceive that I have any right to find fault with it. France was not consulted when we were sent here. Your angry charge, therefore, of our "making a party business of it," is groundless; we had no hand in the business. And, as we neither "acted nor advised" in it, which you suppose, your other high-sounding charge of our doing, thereby, violence to the authority that constituted us, and a great injury and injustice to you, is equally without foundation. As to the concealing it from you, reasons were given by Mr. Deane, that appeared to me satisfactory, and founded entirely on views of public good. I promise to communicate them to you hereafter, if you desire it, that you may have an opportunity of refuting them, if you can. At present, it is not proper.

Your third paragraph, therefore, containing a particular account of what passed between you and me at my house on Monday, seems not to require any answer.

I am still of the same opinion, that, after having sent the treaties themselves by different good conveyances, in which treaties our public character was acknowledged in the most authentic manner, and the avowal of the transaction by the French ambassador to the King of England, which was in all the papers of Europe, the sending a vessel express to carry the news of paying our respects to court, which was likewise in the papers, was an expensive and altogether unnecessary operation.

I received your letter directed to Mr. Deane and myself relating to the accounts. I had no opportunity of showing it to him till the evening of his departure, and then he was in too much of a hurry to peruse it. I could not, therefore, sooner answer it. But I then wrote an answer, acquainting you that he had put into my hands the public papers, with all the information he could give relating to the accounts. It was intended to be transcribed fairly, and sent to you in the morning. Your secretary called for an answer before I had time to copy it. I had a good deal of company; and, thinking a verbal message might perhaps do as well and save the trouble, I desired him, with my compliments, to acquaint you, that I was ready to settle the account with you at any time you should think fit to appoint, except tomorrow, when I should be otherwise engaged. As this verbal message offended you, though I cannot conceive why, I now send you the letter. In it, I complain of your artful, and, I think I may call then, unjust insinuations. You give me fresh instances in the letter I am answering. You magnify your zeal to have the public accounts settled, and insinuate that Mr. Deane and I prevented it, he by "taking possession of all the vouchers," and both of us by taking constantly the public papers to ourselves, which are the property of all the Commissioners.

When this comes to be read in the Committee, for whom it seems to be calculated, rather than for me, who know the circumstances, what can they understand by it, but that you are the only careful, honest man of the three, and that we have some knavish reasons for keeping the accounts in the dark, and you from seeing the vouchers? But the truth is, the papers naturally came into Mr. Deane's hands and mine; first, as he was engaged in the purchasing of goods for the Congress before either you or I came into France; next, as somebody must keep the papers, and you were either on long journeys to Spain, to Vienna and Berlin, or had a commission to go and reside in Spain, which it was expected would soon be executed; whereas Mr. Deane and I lived, almost constantly, in the same house, either at Paris or Passy; you, separate from us; and we did most of the business. Where then could the papers be so properly placed as with us, who had daily occasion to make use of them? I never knew, that you desired to have the keeping of them. You never were refused a paper, or the copy of a paper, that you desired.

As to my not acquainting you with the opportunity of writing to Congress by Mr. Deane, we had lately wrote, and sent, by probably safe conveyances, all I knew of importance to write. I, therefore, did not propose, nor do I write any letter to the Committee by him, especially as in my opinion, considering the route he was to take, he would not arrive so soon as other vessels, which may sail long after him. And he could himself give as good an account of our being at court, the only public transaction since our last letters, as we could write.

You ask me, why I act so inconsistently with my duty to the public? This is a heavy charge, Sir, which I have not deserved. But it is to the public, that I am accountable, and not to you. I have been a servant to many publics, through a long life; have served them with fidelity, and have been honored by their approbation. There is not a single instance of my ever being accused before of acting contrary to their interest or my duty. I shall account to the Congress, when called upon, for this my terrible offence of being silent to you about Mr. Deane's and M. Gérard's departure. And I have no doubt of their equity in acquitting me.

It is true, that I have omitted answering some of your letters, particularly your angry ones, in which you, with very magisterial airs, schooled and documented me, as if I had been one of your domestics. I saw in the strongest light the importance of our living in decent civility towards each other, while our great affairs were depending here. I saw your jealous, suspicious, malignant, and quarrelsome temper, which was daily manifesting itself against Mr. Deane and almost every other person you had any concern with. I, therefore, passed your affronts in silence, did not answer, but burnt your angry letters, and received you, when I next saw you, with the same civility, as if you had never wrote them. Perhaps I may still pursue the same conduct, and not send you these. I believe I shall not, unless exceedingly pressed by you; for, of all things, I hate altercation.

One word more about the accounts. You tell me, that my reason for not settling the accounts before, was, that it was not my business; now, it seemed my business only, and Mr. Deane had nothing to do with it. Both these positions are imaginary. I could never have given any such reasons, being always willing to settle accounts with everybody, and not having the least motive to delay or postpone the settlement of these. Nor could it seem, that I should say Mr. Deane had nothing to do with it. He had done what he could towards it, and, being actually gone, could do no more. The infinity of business we have had is the true and only reason, that I know of, why they have not been settled, that is, why we did not meet, sit down, and compare the vouchers with the articles in the banker's account, in order to see that his charges were supported, and that he had given us due credit for the moneys we had put into his hands. This, I apprehend, is all we have to do here. It is to the Congress we are separately to account for the separate drafts we have made on him. This, Mr. Deane can do, when he arrives, having taken a copy of the account with him.

If you think we should account to one another for our expenses, I have no objection, though I never expected it. I believe they will be found very moderate. I answer mine will, having had only the necessaries of life, and purchased nothing besides, except the *Encyclopædia*, nor sent a sixpence' worth of any thing to my friends or family in America. I have the honor to be your obedient servant.

—B. Franklin

———

He that would live in peace and at ease, Must not speak all he knows, nor judge all he sees.

In a discreet man's mouth a publick thing is private.

A wise Man will desire no more than what he may get justly, use soberly, distribute cheerfully and leave contentedly.

Be temperate in wine, in eating, girls, and cloth, or the Gout will seize you and plague you both.

ON RESOLUTION

From his autobiography, pages 241–243

I had begun in 1733 to study languages; I soon made myself so much a master of the French as to be able to read the books with ease. I then undertook the Italian. An acquaintance, who was also learning it, us'd often to tempt me to play chess with him. Finding this took up too much of the time I had to spare for study, I at length refus'd to play any more, unless on this condition, that the victor in every game should have a right to impose a task, either in parts of the grammar to be got by heart, or in translations, etc., which tasks the vanquish'd was to perform upon honour, before our next meeting. As we play'd pretty equally, we thus beat one another into that language. I afterwards with a little pains-taking, acquir'd as much of the Spanish as to read their books also.

I have already mention'd that I had only one year's instruction in a Latin school, and that when very young, after which I neglected that language entirely. But, when I had attained an acquaintance with the French, Italian, and Spanish, I was surpriz'd to find, on looking over a Latin Testament, that I understood so much more of that language than I had imagined, which encouraged me to apply myself again to the study of it, and I met with more success, as those preceding languages had greatly smooth'd my way.

From these circumstances, I have thought that there is some inconsistency in our common mode of teaching languages. We are told that it is proper to begin first with the Latin, and, having acquir'd that, it will be more easy to attain those modern languages which are deriv'd from it; and yet we do not begin with the Greek, in order more easily to acquire the Latin. It is true that, if you can clamber and get to the top of a staircase without using the steps, you will more easily gain them in descending; but certainly, if you begin with the lowest you will with more ease ascend to the top; and I would therefore offer it to the consideration of those who superintend the education of our youth, whether, since many of those who begin with the Latin quit the same after spending some years without having made any great proficiency, and what they have learnt becomes almost useless, so that their time has been lost, it would not have been better to have begun with the French, proceeding to the Italian, etc.; for, tho', after spending the same time, they should quit the study of languages and never arrive at the Latin, they would, however, have acquired another tongue or two, that, being in modern use, might be serviceable to them in common life.

Who is strong? He that can conquer his bad
Habits.

To err is human, to repent divine; to persist
devilish.

On Frugality and Industry

From his autobiography, pages 91–101

From a child I was fond of reading, and all the little money that came into my hands was ever laid out in books. Pleased with the Pilgrim's Progress, my first collection was of John Bunyan's works in separate little volumes. I afterward sold them to enable me to buy R. Burton's Historical Collections; they were small chapmen's books, and cheap, 40 or 50 in all. My father's little library consisted chiefly of books in polemic divinity, most of which I read, and have since often regretted that, at a time when I had such a thirst for knowledge, more proper books had not fallen in my way, since it was now resolved I should not be a clergyman. Plutarch's *Lives* there was in which I read abundantly, and I still think that time spent to great advantage. There was also a book of

De Foe's, called an *Essay on Projects*, and another of Dr. Mather's, called *Essays to do Good*, which perhaps gave me a turn of thinking that had an influence on some of the principal future events of my life.

This bookish inclination at length determined my father to make me a printer, though he had already one son (James) of that profession. In 1717 my brother James returned from England with a press and letters to set up his business in Boston. I liked it much better than that of my father, but still had a hankering for the sea. To prevent the apprehended effect of such an inclination, my father was impatient to have me bound to my brother. I stood out some time, but at last was persuaded, and signed the indentures when I was yet but twelve years old. I was to serve as an apprentice till I was twenty-one years of age, only I was to be allowed journeyman's wages during the last year. In a little time I made great proficiency in the business, and became a useful hand to my brother. I now had access to better books. An acquaintance with the apprentices of booksellers enabled me sometimes to borrow a small one, which I was careful to return soon and clean. Often I sat up in my room reading the greatest part of the night, when the book was borrowed in the evening and to be returned early in the morning, lest it should be missed or wanted.

And after some time an ingenious tradesman, Mr. Matthew Adams, who had a pretty collection of books, and who frequented our printing-house, took notice of me, invited me to his library, and very kindly lent me such books as I chose to read. I now took a fancy to poetry, and made some little pieces; my brother, thinking it might turn to account, encouraged me, and put me on composing occasional ballads. One was called *The Lighthouse Tragedy*, and contained an account of the drowning of Captain Worthilake, with his two daughters: the other was a sailor's song, on the taking of *Teach* (or Blackbeard) the pirate. They were wretched stuff, in the Grub-street-ballad style; and when they were printed he sent me about the town to sell them. The first sold wonderfully, the event being recent, having made a great noise. This flattered my vanity; but my father discouraged me by ridiculing my performances, and telling me verse-makers were generally beggars. So I escaped being a poet, most probably a very bad one; but as prose writing has been of great use to me in the course of my life, and was a principal means of my advancement, I shall tell you how, in such a situation, I acquired what little ability I have in that way.

There was another bookish lad in the town, John Collins by name, with whom I was intimately acquainted. We sometimes disputed, and very fond we were of argument, and very desirous of confuting one another, which disputatious turn, by the way, is apt to become a very bad habit, making people often extremely disagreeable in company by the contradiction that is necessary to bring it into practice; and thence, besides souring and spoiling the conversation, is productive of disgusts and, perhaps enmities where you may have occasion for friendship. I had caught it by reading my father's books of dispute about religion. Persons of good sense, I have since observed, seldom fall into it, except lawyers, university men, and men of all sorts that have been bred at Edinborough.

A question was once, somehow or other, started between Collins and me, of the propriety of educating the female sex in learning, and their abilities for study. He was of opinion that it was improper, and that they were naturally unequal to it. I took the contrary side, perhaps a little for dispute's sake. He was naturally more eloquent, had a ready plenty of words; and sometimes, as I thought, bore me down more by his fluency than by the strength of his reasons. As we parted without settling the point, and were not to see one another again for some time, I sat down to put my arguments in writing, which I copied fair and sent to him. He answered, and I replied. Three or four letters of a side had passed, when my father happened to find my papers and read them. Without entering into the discussion, he took occasion to talk to me about the manner of my writing; observed that, though I had the advantage of my antagonist in correct spelling and pointing (which I ow'd to the printing-house), I fell far short in elegance of expression, in method and in perspicuity, of which he convinced me by several instances. I saw the justice of his remarks, and thence grew more attentive to the manner in writing, and determined to endeavor at improvement.

About this time I met with an odd volume of the *Spectator*. It was the third. I had never before seen any of them. I bought it, read it over and over, and was much delighted with it. I thought the writing excellent, and wished, if possible, to imitate it. With this view I took some of the papers, and, making short hints of the sentiment in each sentence, laid them by a few days, and then, without looking at the book, try'd to compleat the papers again, by expressing each hinted sentiment at length, and as fully as it had been expressed before, in any suitable words that should come to hand. Then I compared my *Spectator* with the original, discovered some of my faults, and corrected them. But I found I wanted a stock of words, or a readiness in recollecting and using them, which I thought I should have acquired before that time if I had gone on making verses;

since the continual occasion for words of the same import, but of different length, to suit the measure, or of different sound for the rhyme, would have laid me under a constant necessity of searching for variety, and also have tended to fix that variety in my mind, and make me master of it. Therefore I took some of the tales and turned them into verse; and, after a time, when I had pretty well forgotten the prose, turned them back again. I also sometimes jumbled my collections of hints into confusion, and after some weeks endeavored to reduce them into the best order, before I began to form the full sentences and compleat the paper. This was to teach me method in the arrangement of thoughts. By comparing my work afterwards with the original, I discovered many faults and amended them ; but I sometimes had the pleasure of fancying that, in certain particulars of small import, I had been lucky enough to improve the method or the language, and this encouraged me to think I might possibly in time come to be a tolerable English writer, of which I was extreamly ambitious. My time for these exercises and for reading was at night, after work or before it began in the morning, or on Sundays, when I contrived to be in the printing-house alone, evading as much as I could the common attendance on public worship which my father used to exact of me when I was under his care, and which indeed I still thought a duty, though I could not, as it seemed to me, afford time to practise it.

When about 16 years of age I happened to meet with a book, written by one Tryon, recommending a vegetable diet. I determined to go into it. My brother, being yet unmarried, did not keep house, but boarded himself and his apprentices in another family. My refusing to eat flesh occasioned an inconveniency, and I was frequently chid for my singularity. I made myself acquainted with Tryon's manner of preparing some of his dishes, such as boiling potatoes or rice, making hasty pudding, and a few others, and then proposed to my brother, that if he would give me, weekly, half the money he paid for my board, I would board myself. He instantly agreed to it, and I presently found that I could save half what he paid me. This was an additional fund for buying books. But I had another advantage in it. My brother and the rest going from the printing-house to their meals, I remained there alone, and, despatching presently my light repast, which often was no more than a bisket or a slice of bread, a handful of raisins or a tart from the pastry-cook's, and a glass of water, had the rest of the time till their return for study, in which I made the greater progress, from that greater clearness of head and quicker apprehension which usually attend temperance in eating and drinking.

And now it was that, being on some occasion made asham'd of my ignorance in figures, which I had twice failed in learning when at school, I took Cocker's book of Arithmetick, and went through the whole by myself with great ease. I also read Seller's and Shermy's books of Navigation, and became acquainted with the little geometry they contain; but never proceeded far in that science. And I read about this time Locke *on Human Understanding,* and the *Art of Thinking,* by Messrs. du Port Royal.

While I was intent on improving my language, I met with an English grammar (I think it was Greenwood's), at the end of which there were two little sketches of the arts of rhetoric and logic, the latter finishing with a specimen of a dispute in the Socratic method; and soon after I procur'd Xenophon's Memorable Things of Socrates, wherein there are many instances of the same method. I was charm'd with it, adopted it, dropt my abrupt contradiction and positive argumentation, and put on the humble inquirer and doubter. And being then, from reading Shaftesbury and Collins, become a real doubter in many points of our religious doctrine, I found this method safest for myself and very embarassing to those against whom I used it; therefore I took a delight in it, practis'd it continually, and grew very artful and expert in drawing people, even of superior knowledge, into concessions, the consequences of which they did not foresee, entangling them in difficulties out of which they could not extricate themselves, and so obtaining victories that neither myself nor my cause always deserved. I continu'd this method some few years, but gradually left it, retaining only the habit of expressing myself in terms of modest diffidence; never using, when I advanced any thing that may

possibly be disputed, the words *certainly,
undoubtedly,* or any others that give the air
of positiveness to an opinion; but rather say,
I conceive or apprehend a thing to be so and
so; it appears to me, or *I should think it so or
so,* for such and such reasons; or *I imagine it
to be so;* or *it is so, if I am not mistaken.* This
habit, I believe, has been of great advantage to me when I have had occasion to
inculcate my opinions, and persuade men
into measures that I have been from time
to time engag'd in promoting; and, as the
chief ends of conversation are to *inform* or
to be *informed,* to *please* or to *persuade,* I
wish well-meaning, sensible men would not
lessen their power of doing good by a positive, assuming manner, that seldom fails
to disgust, tends to create opposition, and
to defeat every one of those purposes for
which speech was given to us, to wit, giving
or receiving information or pleasure. For, if

you would inform, a positive and dogmatical manner in advancing your sentiments may provoke contradiction and prevent a candid attention. If you wish information and improvement from the knowledge of others, and yet at the same time express yourself as firmly fix'd in your present opinions, modest, sensible men, who do not love disputation, will probably leave you undisturbed in the possession of your error. And by such a manner, you can seldom hope to recommend yourself in *pleasing* your hearers, or to persuade those whose concurrence you desire. Pope says, judiciously:

"Men should be taught as if you taught them not.
And things unknown proposed as things forgot;"

farther recommending to us

> *"To speak, tho' sure, with seeming*
> *diffidence."*

And he might have coupled with this line that which he has coupled with another, I think, less properly,

> "For want of modesty is want of sense."

If you ask, Why less properly? I must repeat the lines,

> "Immodest words admit of no defense,
> For want of modesty is want of sense."

Now, is not *want of sense* (where a man is so unfortunate as to want it) some apology for his *want of modesty?* and would not the lines stand more justly thus?

> "Immodest words admit *but* this defense,
> That want of modesty is want of sense."

This, however, I should submit to better judgments.

———

Industry, Perseverance, & Frugality,
make Fortune yield.

If you know how to spend less than you get,
you have the philosopher's stone.

ON SINCERITY AND JUSTICE

From his autobiography, pages 164–167

Before I enter upon my public appearance in business, it may be well to let you know the then state of my mind with regard to my principles and morals, that you may see how far those influenc'd the future events of my life. My parents had early given me religious impressions, and brought me through my childhood piously in the Dissenting way. But I was scarce fifteen, when, after doubting by turns of several points, as I found them disputed in the different books I read, I began to doubt of Revelation itself. Some books against Deism fell into my hands; they were said to be the substance of sermons preached at Boyle's Lectures. It happened that they wrought an effect on me quite contrary to what was intended by them; for the arguments of the

Deists, which were quoted to be refuted, appeared to me much stronger than the refutations; in short, I soon became a thorough Deist. My arguments perverted some others, particularly Collins and Ralph; but, each of them having afterwards wrong'd me greatly without the least compunction, and recollecting Keith's conduct towards me (who was another freethinker), and my own towards Vernon and Miss Read, which at times gave me great trouble, I began to suspect that this doctrine, tho' it might be true, was not very useful. My London pamphlet, which had for its motto these lines of Dryden:

"Whatever is, is right. Though purblind man
Sees but a part o' the chain, the nearest link:
His eyes not carrying to the equal beam,
That poises all above;"

and from the attributes of God, his infinite wisdom, goodness and power, concluded that nothing could possibly be wrong in the world, and that vice and virtue were empty distinctions, no such things existing, appear'd now not so clever a performance as I once thought it; and I doubted whether some error had not insinuated itself unperceiv'd into my argument, so as to infect all that follow'd, as is common in metaphysical reasonings.

I grew convinc'd that *truth, sincerity* and *integrity* in dealings between man and man were of the utmost importance to the felicity of life; and I form'd written resolutions, which still remain in my journal book, to practice them ever while I lived. Revelation had indeed no weight with me, as such; but I entertain'd an opinion that, though certain actions might not be bad *because* they were forbidden by it, or good *because* it commanded them, yet probably those actions might be forbidden *because* they were bad for us, or commanded *because* they were beneficial to us, in their own natures, all the circumstances of things considered. And this persuasion, with the kind hand of Providence, or some guardian angel, or accidental favorable circumstances and situations, or all together, preserved me, thro' this dangerous time of youth, and the hazardous situations I was sometimes in among strangers, remote from the eye and advice of my father, without any willful gross immorality or injustice, that might have been expected from my want of religion. I say willful, because the instances I have mentioned had something of *necessity* in them, from my youth, inexperience, and the knavery of others. I had therefore a tolerable character to begin the world with; I valued it properly, and determin'd to preserve it.

———

If thou injures conscience, it will have
its revenge on thee.

When you're good to others, you are best
to your self.

Act uprightly and despise Calumny;
Dirt may stick to a Mud Wall, but not to
polish'd Marble.

The honest Man takes Pains, and then
enjoys Pleasures; the knave takes Pleasures,
and then suffers Pains.

ON CLEANLINESS AND ORDER

From his autobiography, pages 285–292

Our city, tho' laid out with a beautifull regularity, the streets large, strait, and crossing each other at right angles, had the disgrace of suffering those streets to remain long unpav'd, and in wet weather the wheels of heavy carriages plough'd them into a quagmire, so that it was difficult to cross them; and in dry weather the dust was offensive. I had liv'd near what was call'd the Jersey Market, and saw with pain the inhabitants wading in mud while purchasing their provisions. A strip of ground down the middle of that market was at length pav'd with brick, so that, being once in the market, they had firm footing, but were often over shoes in dirt to get there. By talking and writing on the subject, I was at length instrumental in getting the street pav'd with stone between the market and the brick'd foot-pavement, that was on each side next the houses. This, for some time, gave an easy access to the market dry-shod; but, the rest of the street not being pav'd, whenever a carriage came out of the mud upon this pavement, it shook off and left its dirt upon it, and it was soon cover'd with mire, which was not remov'd, the city as yet having no scavengers.

After some inquiry, I found a poor, industrious man, who was willing to undertake keeping the pavement clean, by sweeping it twice a week, carrying off the dirt from before all the neighbours' doors, for the sum of sixpence per month, to be paid by each house. I then wrote and printed a paper setting forth the advantages to the neighbourhood that might be obtain'd by this small expense; the greater ease in keeping our houses clean, so much dirt not being brought in by people's feet; the benefit to the shops by more custom, etc., etc., as buyers could more easily get at them; and by not having, in windy weather, the dust blown in upon their goods, etc., etc. I sent one of these papers to each house, and in a day or two went round to see who would subscribe an agreement to pay these sixpences; it was unanimously sign'd, and for a time well executed. All the inhabitants of the city were delighted with the cleanliness of the pavement that surrounded the market, it being a convenience to all, and this rais'd a general desire to have all the streets paved, and made the people more willing to submit to a tax for that purpose.

After some time I drew a bill for paving the city, and brought it into the Assembly. It was just before I went to England, in 1757, and did not pass till I was gone, and then with an alteration in the mode of assessment, which I thought not for the better, but with an additional provision for lighting as well as paving the streets, which was a great improvement. It was by a private person, the late Mr. John Clifton, his giving a sample of the utility of lamps, by placing one at his door, that the people were first impress'd with the idea of enlighting all the city. The honour of this public benefit has also been ascrib'd to me, but it belongs truly to that gentleman. I did but follow his example, and have only some merit to claim respecting the form of our lamps, as differing from the globe lamps we were at first supply'd with from London. Those we found inconvenient in these respects: they admitted no air below; the smoke, therefore, did not readily go out above, but circulated in the globe, lodg'd on its inside, and soon obstructed the light they were intended to afford; giving, besides, the daily trouble of wiping them clean; and an accidental stroke on one of them would demolish it, and render it totally useless. I therefore suggested the composing them of four flat panes, with a long funnel above to draw up the smoke, and crevices admitting air below, to facilitate the ascent of the smoke; by this means they were kept clean, and did not grow dark in a few hours, as the London lamps do, but continu'd bright till morning, and an accidental stroke would generally break but a single pane, easily repair'd.

I have sometimes wonder'd that the Londoners did not, from the effect holes in the bottom of the globe lamps us'd at Vauxhall have in keeping them clean, learn to have such holes in their street lamps. But, these holes being made for another purpose, viz., to communicate flame more suddenly to the wick by a little flax hanging down thro' them, the other use, of letting in air, seems not to have been thought of; and therefore, after the lamps have been lit a few hours, the

streets of London are very poorly illumi-
nated.

The mention of these improvements
puts me in mind of one I propos'd, when in
London, to Dr. Fothergill, who was among
the best men I have known, and a great
promoter of useful projects. I had observ'd
that the streets, when dry, were never
swept, and the light dust carried away; but
it was suffer'd to accumulate till wet weather
reduc'd it to mud, and then, after lying some
days so deep on the pavement that there
was no crossing but in paths kept clean by
poor people with brooms, it was with great
labour rak'd together and thrown up into
carts open above, the sides of which suffer'd
some of the slush at every jolt on the pavement to shake out and fall, sometimes to the
annoyance of foot-passengers. The reason
given for not sweeping the dusty streets was,

that the dust would fly into the windows of shops and houses.

An accidental occurrence had instructed me how much sweeping might be done in a little time. I found at my door in Craven-street, one morning, a poor woman sweeping my pavement with a birch broom; she appeared very pale and feeble, as just come out of a fit of sickness. I ask'd who employ'd her to sweep there; she said, "Nobody; but I am very poor and in distress, and I sweeps before gentlefolkses doors, and hopes they will give me something." I bid her sweep the whole street clean, and I would give her a shilling; this was at nine o'clock; at 12 she came for the shilling. From the slowness I saw at first in her working, I could scarce believe that the work was done so soon, and sent my servant to examine it, who reported that the whole street was swept perfectly clean, and all the dust plac'd in the gutter, which was in the middle; and the next rain wash'd it quite away, so that the pavement and even the kennel were perfectly clean.

I then judg'd that, if that feeble woman could sweep such a street in three hours, a strong, active man might have done it in half the time. And here let me remark the convenience of having but one gutter in such a narrow street, running down its middle, instead of two, one on each side, near the footway; for where all the rain that falls on a street runs from the sides and meets in the middle, it forms there a current strong enough to wash away all the mud it meets with; but when divided into two channels, it is often too weak to cleanse either, and only makes the mud it finds more fluid, so that the wheels of carriages and feet of horses throw and dash it upon the foot-pavement, which is thereby rendered foul and slippery, and sometimes splash it upon those who are walking. My proposal, communicated to the good doctor, was as follows:

"For the more effectual cleaning and keeping clean the streets of London and Westminster, it is proposed that the several watchmen be contracted with to have the dust swept up in dry seasons, and the mud rak'd up at other times, each in the several streets and lanes of his round; that they be furnish'd with brooms and other proper instruments for these purposes, to be kept at their respective stands, ready to furnish the poor people they may employ in the service.

"That in the dry summer months the dust be all swept up into heaps at proper distances, before the shops and windows of houses are usually opened, when the scavengers, with close-covered carts, shall also carry it all away.

"That the mud, when rak'd up, be not left in heaps to be spread abroad again by the wheels of carriages and trampling of horses, but that the scavengers be provided with bodies of carts, not plac'd high upon wheels, but low upon sliders, with lattice bottoms, which, being cover'd with straw, will retain the mud thrown into them, and permit the water to drain from it, whereby it will become much lighter, water making the greatest part of its weight; these bodies of carts to be plac'd at convenient distances, and the mud brought to them in wheelbarrows; they remaining where plac'd till the mud is drain'd, and then horses brought to draw them away."

I have since had doubts of the practicability of the latter part of this proposal, on account of the narrowness of some streets, and the difficulty of placing the draining-sleds so as not to encumber too much the passage; but I am still of opinion that the former, requiring the dust to be swept up and carry'd away before the shops are open, is very practicable in the summer, when the days are long; for, in walking thro' the Strand and Fleet-street one morning at seven o'clock, I observ'd there was not one shop open, tho' it had been daylight and the sun up above three hours; the inhabitants of London chusing voluntarily to live much by candle-light, and sleep by sunshine, and yet often complain, a little absurdly, of the duty on candles, and the high price of tallow.

Some may think these trifling matters not worth minding or relating; but when they consider that tho' dust blown into the eyes of a single person, or into a single shop on a windy day, is but of small importance, yet the great number of the instances in a populous city, and its frequent repetitions give it weight and consequence, perhaps they will not censure very severely those who bestow some attention to affairs of this seemingly low nature. Human felicity is produc'd not so much by great pieces of good fortune that seldom happen, as by little advantages that occur every day. Thus, if you teach a poor young man to shave himself, and keep his razor in order, you may contribute more to the happiness of his life than in giving him a thousand guineas. The money may be soon spent, the regret only remaining of having foolishly consumed it; but in the other case, he escapes the frequent vexation of waiting for barbers, and of their sometimes dirty fingers, offensive breaths, and dull razors; he shaves when most convenient to him, and enjoys daily the pleasure of its being done with a good instrument. With these sentiments I have hazarded the few preceding pages, hoping they may afford hints which some time or other may be useful to a city I love, having lived many years in it very happily, and perhaps to some of our towns in America.

———

Clean your Finger, before you point at my Spots.

He that lies down with dogs, shall rise up with fleas.

Honours change manners.

To God we owe fear and love; to our neighbours justice and charity; to our selves prudence and sobriety.

ON CHASTITY AND TRANQUILITY

From his autobiography, pages 189–192

I had hitherto continu'd to board with Godfrey, who lived in part of my house with his wife and children, and had one side of the shop for his glazier's business, tho' he worked little, being always absorbed in his mathematics. Mrs. Godfrey projected a match for me with a relation's daughter, took opportunities of bringing us often together, till a serious courtship on my part ensu'd, the girl being in herself very deserving. The old folks encourag'd me by continual invitations to supper, and by leaving us together, till at length it was time to explain. Mrs. Godfrey manag'd our little treaty. I let her know that I expected as much money with their daughter as would pay off my remaining debt for the printing-house, which I believe was not then above a hundred pounds. She brought me word they had no such sum to spare; I said they might mortgage their house in the loan-office. The answer to this, after some days, was, that they did not approve the match; that, on inquiry of Bradford, they had been inform'd the printing business was not a profitable one; the types would soon be worn out, and more wanted; that S. Keimer and D. Harry had failed one after the other, and I should probably soon follow them; and, therefore, I was forbidden the house, and the daughter shut up.

Whether this was a real change of sentiment or only artifice, on a supposition of our being too far engaged in affection to retract, and therefore that we should steal a marriage, which would leave them at liberty to give or withhold what they pleas'd, I know not; but I suspected the latter, resented it, and went no more. Mrs. Godfrey brought me afterward some more favorable accounts of their disposition, and would have drawn me on again; but I declared absolutely my resolution to have nothing more to do with that family. This was resented by the Godfreys; we differ'd, and they removed, leaving me the whole house, and I resolved to take no more inmates.

But this affair having turned my thoughts to marriage, I look'd round me and made overtures of acquaintance in other places; but soon found that, the business of a printer being generally thought a poor one, I was not to expect money with a wife, unless with such a one as I should not otherwise think agreeable. In the mean time, that hard-to-be-governed passion of youth hurried me frequently into intrigues with low women that fell in my way, which were attended with some expense and great inconvenience, besides a continual risque to my health by a distemper which of all things I dreaded, though by great good luck I escaped it. A friendly correspondence as neighbors and old acquaintances had continued between me and Mrs. Read's family, who all had a regard for me from the time of my first lodging in their house. I was often invited there and consulted in their affairs, wherein I sometimes was of service. I piti'd poor Miss Read's unfortunate situation, who was generally dejected, seldom cheerful, and avoided company. I considered my giddiness and inconstancy when in London as in a great degree the cause of her unhappiness, tho' the mother was good enough to think the fault more her own than mine, as she had prevented our marrying before I went thither, and persuaded the other match in my absence. Our mutual affection was revived, but there were now great objections to our union. The match was indeed looked upon as invalid, a preceding wife being said to be living in England; but this could not easily be prov'd, because of the distance; and, tho' there was a report of his death, it was not certain. Then, tho' it should be true, he had left many debts, which his successor might be call'd upon to pay. We ventured, however, over all these difficulties, and I took her to wife, September 1st, 1730. None of the inconveniences happened that we had apprehended; she proved a good and faithful helpmate, assisted me much by attending the shop; we throve together, and have ever mutually endeavor'd to make each other happy. Thus I corrected that great *erratum* as well as I could.

———

You cannot pluck roses without fears of thorns,
Nor enjoy a fair wife without danger of horns.

When ♂ and ♀ in conjunction lie,
Then, maids, whate'er is ask'd of you, deny.

Hear no ill of a friend, nor speak any of an
enemy.

He that doth what he should not, shall feel
what he would not.

ON HUMILITY

From his autobiography, pages 68–74

Hereby, too, I shall indulge the inclination so natural in old men, to be talking of themselves and their own past actions; and I shall indulge it without being tiresome to others, who, through respect to age, might conceive themselves obliged to give me a hearing, since this may be read or not as any one pleases. And, lastly (I may as well confess it, since my denial of it will be believed by nobody), perhaps I shall a good deal gratify my own *vanity*. Indeed, I scarce ever heard or saw the introductory words, "*Without vanity I may say,*" &c, but some vain thing immediately followed. Most people dislike vanity in others, whatever share they have of it themselves; but I give it fair quarter wherever I meet with it, being persuaded that it is often productive of good to the possessor, and to others that are within his sphere of action; and therefore, in many cases, it would not be altogether absurd if a man were to thank God for his vanity among the other comforts of life.

And now I speak of thanking God, I desire with all humility to acknowledge that I owe the mentioned happiness of my past life to His kind providence, which lead me to the means I used and gave them success. My belief of this induces me to *hope,* though I must not *presume,* that the same goodness will still be exercised toward me, in continuing that happiness, or enabling me to bear a fatal reverse, which I may experience as others have done; the complexion of my future fortune being known to Him only in whose power it is to bless to us even our afflictions.

Declaiming against Pride, is not always a sign of Humility.

None but the well-bred man knows how to confess a fault, or acknowledge himself in an error.

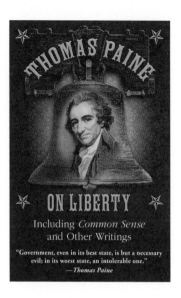

Thomas Paine on Liberty
Including *Common Sense* and Other Writings
Thomas Paine

Thomas Paine is most famous for writing *Common Sense,* a pamphlet distributed during the American Revolution advocating for colonial America's independence from Great Britain. Now, collected here in a beautiful gift book volume are excerpts from this important historical American document, as well as several of his other writings.

Paine believed in more than just freedom in the form of revolution and overthrowing governments. He also believed in freedom from oppressive and organized religions and monopolies. Included in this book are passages taken from The Age of Reason and The Rights of Man, as well as letters to George Washington, Benjamin Rush, and Samuel Adams, and pamphlets such as "The American Crisis" and "Agrarian Justice." Throughout his writings, Paine provides excellent and timeless wisdom on attaining liberty and living a democratic life.

$9.95 Hardcover • 144 pages

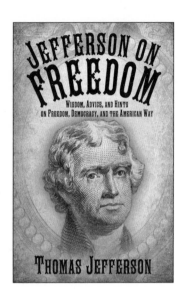

Jefferson on Freedom
Wisdom, Advice, and Hints on Freedom, Democracy,
and the American Way
Thomas Jefferson

Thomas Jefferson is most famous for the writing of the Declaration of
Independence, which espouses the general principles of freedom and
democracy that Americans hold dear. Now, collected here for the first
time, is this historical American document, as well as several of his other
famous writings. Included in this book are excerpts from his only full-
length book, *Notes on the State of Virginia*, letters to Samual Kercheval and
Edward Carrington on liberal democracy and freedom, an exchange
with Danbury Baptists regarding the right to religious freedom, and
his manual on parliamentary policy. Jefferson provides excellent and
timeless quotes on attaining freedom and living a democratic life.

$9.95 Hardcover • 144 pages

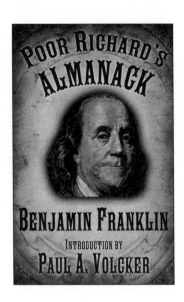

Poor Richard's Almanack
Benjamin Franklin
Introduction by Paul A. Volcker

Benjamin Franklin's classic book is full of timeless, thought-provoking insights that are as valuable today as they were over two centuries ago. With more than 700 pithy proverbs, Franklin lays out the rules everyone should live by and offers advice on such subjects as money, friendship, marriage, ethics, and human nature. They range from the famous "A penny saved is a penny earned" to the lesser-known but equally practical "When the wine enters, out goes the truth." Other truisms like "Fish and visitors stink after three days" combine sharp wit with wisdom. Paul Volcker's new introduction offers a fascinating perspective on Franklin's beloved work.

$9.95 Hardcover • 96 pages

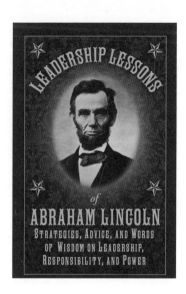

Leadership Lessons of Abraham Lincoln
Strategies, Advice, and Words of Wisdom on
Leadership, Responsibility, and Power

In *Leadership Lessons of Abraham Lincoln*, the best, most thought-
provoking, and inspiring excerpts from Lincoln's speeches and writings
have been collected in an effort to help today's business leaders apply
his principles to their own work and life. While it may not always be
easy to follow Honest Abe's sterling example, the lessons one learns
from reading this book are sure to inspire and give rise to some deep
contemplation about the role of the leader in organizations both small
and large, and reaffirm one's faith in the principles Lincoln held so
deeply.

$9.95 Hardcover • 128 pages

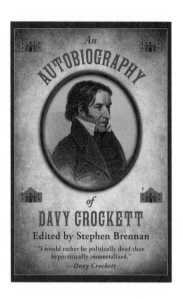

An Autobiography of Davy Crockett
Edited by Stephen Brennan

Based in part on Davy Crockett's own writings, this is the true story of one of America's most iconic historical figures. From his days as a scout for Andrew Jackson during the war of 1812, his time as a congressman for the state of Tennessee, and his eventual death at the Alamo, Davy Crockett led a life that was admired and idealized by people all across America, to this very day. Read about the monopolist and corporate misdeeds, environmental degradation, and foreign military adventures that he battled during his amazing life. Illustrated with drawings and photos, discover the rich history—part myth and part fact—behind this great American man.

$12.95 Hardcover • 320 pages